T0367073

RAG

Also by Julie Carr

Poetry

Mead: An Epithalamion (University of Georgia Press)
Equivocal (Alice James Books)
100 Notes on Violence (Ahsahta Press)
Sarah-Of Fragments and Lines (Coffee House Books)

Criticism

Surface Tension: Ruptural Time and the Poetics of Desire in Late Victorian Poetry (Dalkey Archive)

RAG

JULIE CARR

OMNIDAWN PUBLISHING
RICHMOND, CALIFORNIA
2014

Original cover art by Luther Price, "Earthly Delights," 2012, courtesy of Luther Price, Callicoon Fine Arts, NY, and CIRCUS, Berlin.

Book cover and interior design by Cassandra Smith

Offset printed in the United States
by Edwards Brothers Malloy, Ann Arbor, Michigan
On 55# Enviro Natural 100% Recycled 100% PCW
Acid Free Archival Quality FSC Certified Paper
with Rainbow FSC Certified Colored End Papers

Library of Congress Cataloging-in-Publication Data

Carr, Julie, 1966-
[Poems. Selections]
Rag / Julie Carr.
pages cm
ISBN 978-1-890650-93-3 (trade pbk. : alk. paper)
I. Title.
PS3603.A77425R35 2014
811'.6--dc23

2013045788

Published by Omnidawn Publishing, Richmond, California
www.omnidawn.com (510) 237-5472 (800) 792-4957
10 9 8 7 6 5 4 3 2 1
ISBN: 978-1-890650-93-3

I wonder if this new reality is going to destroy me.

- Barbara Guest

Inhuman actors bright new animals

Give orders to tamed men

Earth

O Tattered-one the rivers mend you

- Apollinaire

—from out of the wretched tide through the heat mothers pass—

It's always that the lines of color are too stark

So how can I place a hand there, there on the edge of a truck?

One's body is in response

But today my face grows smaller

I want the narrative of walking to a bus

Alcohol sped to my eyelids

How power moves when hidden underground

A red flag marks buried electricity

But I'd thought it was buried everywhere

On November 17 and in summer

The letter carrier in his cap

I could find just one of my slippers

Nonetheless I put it on my foot

A wasp lay dead on my desk

The majority opinion was against

My "vacation" my "shadow" my "vacation"

When will I learn to be the author of my own invention?

This from the spider descending the shade

When a man puts his hand on my waist

Nothing left in my cup or my word bank

I "refuse" I am "bribed" I "refuse"

But am good with the liquefaction process

A brutal response

I could hear you speaking in the alley

Where the girl in the lavender vest would come and go

And he who grows basil each summer

Hangs his jeans out to dry

Love is no way to be removed

Static on the whip of the day

—"I was drinking / I was drunken / I was written in"—

I think resin into the wine. I mean to speak of the future. The world within her shoulders. A place I am afraid to touch. My child is a lover of music. Buoyant in her pursuit. Of the snow the grasses beneath the snow the treble clef. In this document of my intentions I will create a puppet for my girl. And so I evoke the name of my mother, the name of my childhood friend. I feel as if a residue adhering to a rim. As if I am only reflexive. A melody drawn down from the avenue casts its voluptuous swell against the doors. Doors of the house, fence around the school—higher than any child could climb. One by one the old senators retire, while the youngest girl sits up in bed. A tongue of flame upon her head. A near park of meek trees shudders. Sink reason into rhyme. For my mother sleeps chemical and my mother sleeps broken.

The cracked lip of the cup reminds me what I meant when I swore upon the black earth my allegiance.

—a tress—a fidget in the chest. Twist of nerve talking me—

And if I grow sick in public

it's only to offer up my "purple well"

Tuesday's well

to the pallid child, to the brother, the crowd

When the gathering tightens around me

that way shortening my hem

this is the pleasure I am after

because of how it swells in me made

—A pink—from a trench—tryst of breath and sweat—

—as horrified you see yourself invented—

And we with eyes averted sat by the crying woman. Resting elbows on our knees in a posture of care/disregard. Just as on a plane a woman three rows back, seated between two suited men, suddenly began to sob—loud and unabashed, not bothering to wipe her tears, not covering her face, just sitting staring forward, wailing like a baby. No one said anything. Not the men—one gazed out the window, the other continued to read his screen as if nothing—not the attendants, who did not come. Now in heavy spring snow, a tree loses a limb. And we are glad—an opening where was a thing. Then she stops crying and her face clears to resemble the sidewalk beside the DMV. Without anything to create shade, anything at all, the people come and go—

their apprehended tasks lit by a limitless seasonless fire.

—face does not adjust itself—

—then she stops crying—

—and “all your care is radiant”?—

At the present time, a city opens itself to rain and to farmworkers in their trucks, but not to the man who lit himself on fire in the greenhouse, his son down the road playing with the neighbor's son.

Smoking a cigarette down the alley, a woman carries her groceries home. My friend on his porch watches the cars park below, backing into their spots with such confidence it astounds him. Good breeze arrives and what are we to do with that, that news and that—that photograph of fire? Living along the borders of roads. At dinner our friend says, "I figure business as usual is the best approach." She means to dying, which might now define her or us. The kids won't eat, not one of them; instead, faces flushed from running, riding bikes around the neighborhood, or putting on their death costumes with a cowboy hat, their ghost costumes with a blanket. And if being here is listening to a bird respond to the warming of the earth in the early spring. And if scissors and pencils mean I've got myself ready for making and destroying, ready for marking and scoring, what not sleeping portends is a kind of edge to the day, a folded edge so something is always hidden in that fold. A city resembles a forest, resembles a factory, a body. Of a dog. Where that head on that lap is a kind of talisman against the burning of a father, of a husband.

One spies in the grocery store an old man stalled at the cereal, deciding, an old woman with efficient methods for carrying. And if I beg here. A cry pens wreck and truck, tile and fur. This prying sun on the door makes a target. Her groceries home.

*

In the paper, the funeral of a boy. Yes, I am afraid, says one friend. Another writes, "I don't know how to think about it," though in fact he writes "tink"—I don't know how to tink about it. For months I return to the same book every morning, the same lines, but each time it's as if I've never read them. The words renew themselves in the night like sleeping children. A city reveals itself never. When we first arrived, dual-family homes fronted with chain-link. Someone's belongings out for sale or display or pick-up. Pairs of shoes in a line on a blanket. Plastic bowls and cooking utensils. Car parts, lamps. The houses undressing. A city is decorated by its bridges. White and arching like the

sincerity of summer heat.

In the paper, the funeral of a boy. Each participant has his or her hand to his or her mouth. The girl bounds towards me across a field. Let me tell you everything, she says, talking rapidly through her thirst. School lets out at three and from the doors, floods of kids. From the buses, they pour down. Water's what's needed here. In the paper a man who's lost his face to fire—no eyebrows, nose, or lips—is given a new face off a donor. The new face is complete with muscles and nerves and will function on its own, as his own. Happiness, says my son, is like new blood, like getting a bucket of new blood. Each time I am happy, I receive the new blood. Arriving at the bookstore in spring.

*

For days and days after her death I have a headache. I am surprised to realize it's been over a month. Since her death. Since her death, another friend's prognosis is very bad. Her five years (if she's lucky) left in her body will be spent doing what she's always done, "business as usual." Tim witnesses an accident on 17th in which a woman driving an SUV hits a six-year-old girl. Arriving home, he's crying and the girls are crying, though they don't know why. Because her eyes were open, he's sure the girl is dead. The truth is, he tells Alice, she had no fear. But, we learn later, she's not dead, or may not be dead, we do not and cannot know. This is only the beginning.

*

A city opens itself to rain and to farmworkers in their trucks. Smoking a cigarette in an elevator the woman lets her grocery bag lean against her leg. Present tense owns such pure confidence on the porch. And what are we to do with that fire? The best or better approach to dying is business and rest, or face flushed and running? Dressing in your death costume with your blanket warming the earth in early spring both marks and scores the edge of the day. A city resembles a resting dog, its head on the lap of that father or husband. A city is an efficient way of carrying. And if I beg here, a cry pens itself toward the prying sun. A target. A wretch. The cars parked each morning like lines from a poem always the same and always misremembered. Each night the cars renew themselves like sleeping children.

*

Car parts and lamps, the houses undressing, the white backs of bridges, and every participant has his hand to his mouth. To find a place of rest, a place not busy with men, I walk. To workers in their smoking, to women on their legs. Dressed in their death costumes they mark and score the city, and each night, sleeping children just a little bit revealed, exposing their blank backs, their thirst. A man with a new face and a bucket of new blood hits a girl on the avenue.

That running in death costumes; that city like a dog in the sun.

—in the sincerity of summer heat—

—a citizen among you—

In crayon drawings

Some persons lie buried in fire and some have been suspended in a wave

Rain withdraws its praise

I'm unable to rest, her hunger crying through a vent

I wanted to unzip her coat, to slide a hand

Under the body of a car

But I was never one to fix a machine. Elsewhere the nest of the wasp

Other, the birch-bark and lichen

The townhouses stunned by foreclosure

The bubbling well in the mall

Now are we wanting plaster surrogates

To gather nightly in our halls?

"Like a maelstrom with a notch"

This world can dizzy even a womb

And mine is just a bit of breathing

A bit of breathing through a line

Not because I'm humble, because I'm made

Made to be humiliated and to be adored

I've never until now sensed two terms

To stand closer together than these

To gather nightly in our erosions

Our data bases our platforms our diagrams

If that's how you want to think about it

If that's how you want to think about it

In the blue dusted dawn of a feast day

I'm certain to dissolve in the fever

Of what pours from your skull, officious sun

—but is grieving a politics?—

—a civic lyric on the house floor—

Some men

I don't much

read them

Prefer the straddled fissures

in which the animal is most famished and most indolent

Though I have answered your questions about the molestation of children
and have offered a definition of rape

Though I have invented a blue-skinned bath-witch who turns your
　　　　bathwater to ice
and a benevolent squirrel who after spying through the window,
spirals down a tree to find your

mother, I have no true gifts beyond the gift of placing the pieces one
beside another all day and all night

until you wake up and I yank at your hair

With my brush

—her face cannot adjust itself into yolk or flag—

—neither one nor none—

—to be fucked in the fruits of some labor—

The sensation of a "beyond" is an effect of consciousness: except when sleeping

or for the not yet born

whose subject is itself

My country likes the torso gendered female, anyone's hands, male necks, and

baby eyes

Garrulous and piqued, live candles in phase transition as the
cold comes running through piles of kid clothes
or Emily scrawls her name in crayon across the table.
Sweltering messages in wine glasses fallow, I go running or trudging
with my gates wide open and all investments pay for themselves in the end
though the apartment is unsellable, or sellable only at a reduced price
which might make you fall backward onto your head, your hoodie
a bit of a cushion but not enough, eat your chicken.
Red in the flash drive the marker top the vaginal wall the sleeper whose foot I shake—

—"And what is knowledge in this condition?"—

Then, this male eyebrow—tense curve of doubt

is scanned so easily with my finger, inexorable stroke, flames drawing upward,
toward the geese who efficiently re-gather their fundamental geometry

They seek an attentive reader with the tight scruples of devotion

"And so I began to consider history"

Everyone has a cousin like Sam

I've got to get out of here

Swinging on a gate

Whose theater is it now?

No, she didn't "mount him," she took a bullet

A white girl and a boy entered a field. One of them was in a lot of pain. The pain began in the belly, spreading into the shoulders and arms and down even into the legs. Because of this pain, the white girl and boy walked slowly, holding hands. A few steps, and then stop. A few more, stop. Whenever they stopped the one in pain would only breathe. The other would look up into the mobile sky, down at the grass or over toward the trees. And then, when the one who was in pain could move again, they'd resume. They walked in order to cross a field, but the field was long and it seemed the trees receded. The trees receded but not the pain, which returned again and again, each time very old. Every field has a goat. Bleating or bleeding in a hazy distance, with lilies and flies.

A white boy felt the weight in his pocket. He called that weight his freedom and he cooked it. He walked with a lean to the left, for the freedom was heavy. Circled a car, circled a traffic light. He was losing air like a balloon drifting down. Hot on the thigh, which was what he wanted. Some heat. Breeze in the face carried salt but not only. Salt from the sea and fat from the fryer. He was a boy, he could wear no makeup; no lipstick turned his mouth to ruddy. To find a color in this boy you had to split him open. And all his holes were tight. A girl saw him turning circles with his freedom. She narrowed her eyes and blurred him out. Now just smudge of pale: a haunt, a mote, a fiction.

My country, said the boy to the girl, likes its children shot through

My country, said the girl to the boy, likes its women weighted or flayed

My country, said the boy, tears away. We've never really loved the human.

A mother's

just a wisp

And now my hope is drunk: a thought in which I do not have a face

My presence, most of all, a discharge

—in the parked car, sleeping just
a little bit revealed—

So am a conduit for money—while in the pool turning

At the same time a conduit for

water, dioxins, lead

The dog pressed his face against my thigh. Window gives fact of the air

stationed at the brick wall nine

inches away

I eat salt

purchase debt

I had thought crossing the bridge would deliver me to the woman's face, her filmed face with its waves of regret. But during the decades when people always ate a hot lunch, a woman at night in a park alone was criminal, even if crying. I thought about his weaker character stuck in some army fatigues but replete with live particularity, his hand, for instance. While the male carries an epic weight, the female in the film simply scrubs it off, running through rain. To anyone living in it, war would seem "vague, confused, atmospheric," though not at home. This is how her face was like my own: I also wanted to be looked at like a hole is, a hole in the road, the garden, or sky. There were gaps between her teeth and she grinned ghoulishly at her own reflection in the moving train window.

There are a few ways to read this shot. For dreaming of the body of an ex-lover when one's husband is out of range might suggest a longing not for the other but for the absent one, the one who cannot be reached, while in the mirror every night, the face more and more a woman's who has absorbed the devotion of two girls into her skin. Then, there is the phantom shot. We share much in common. There is something here about trying to subsume behavior within the rule, and what else is a line of verse but a casting and recasting of the inside of the body?

Consider my identity, she might say, failing to force her reflection to still. But no one likes a boaster.

Lying awake at night could be a signal of guilt, could mean the woman has placed her desires first, has gone "shopping" and been to "the movies." Mountains visible between foregrounded trees, she tries to breathe into an acceleration as her husband maintains his attachment to the crossword. These vague hours will deliver us eventually to the speech about the war. Reading a book on a bench, she hopes fervently for a withdrawal. This kind of enthusiasm has no real place in the afternoon's re-gathering of kids, just as self-abandon finds little place in the law. Within the doctrine of unclean hands, her shame is made clear as a metallic ringing in the ear.

—and if I beg here, O hole—

—Let me tell you everything, rapidly through my thirst—

Or should I submit my file to revision—allow each line to reemerge as if a bee from the mortar or ant from the socket—

If, as a child, I saw myself reflected in the lens of his glasses, saw my elongated face like the portrait of a saint in a portico—

The "advancement community" includes every eleven-year-old girl with her tongue in her mouth, her hair yanked back

"Like an oxen yoked" the daughter must please the king, please or be killed. For the king said, "come to me not clothed, not naked, not riding, not walking, not in the road, and not off the road, and if you can do that I will marry you"

"It is not the act of a judicious man," said the brother, "to let what is valuable leave his house"

A woman might be a kind of postproduction medium, or a filter through which the desires in the ground are felt

Buried to her chin in dirt, the dirt made out of her own skin, does she play the waves of her spit on her tongue, spit mixed into that dirt?

"So she went away, put off everything she had on, and then she was not clothed. Took a great fishing net, seated herself in it and wrapped it entirely round and round her, so that she was not naked. And she hired an ass, tied the fisherman's net to its tail, so that it was forced to drag her along, and that was neither riding

nor walking. The ass had also to drag her in the ruts, so that she only touched the ground with her big toe, and that was neither being in the road nor off the road. And when she arrived in that fashion, the king said she had guessed the riddle and fulfilled all the conditions"

She blushed and blanched, for she never thought that her brother would try to give her a couple of rotten eggs when he had a hundred fresh ones

"Ass or billy goat, what kind of stew is this? Am I your sister or just oily cheese?"

"But what is it you like about me?" she asked him a month later. "Your hands," he said, "when they serve me the sweets." And so the sister cut off her hands, just as St. Lucy gouged out her eyes, offering them on a cake plate

Her hair a ratty mess, her head fully nits, her temples plucked. Her nose a knotty bump, her forehead like a hammer, her tits saddlebags. But her mother loved her

as if pure from the archive

And yet, as soon as the day presented the paintbrushes of its rays, the father took the little girl by the hand and delivered her as a gift

to the sun

—now have we become archaic?—

—within the doctrine of unclean hands—

—a ringing in the ear—

A technician provides a service while the law prescribes a border, a border around the language to frighten you. In this way we conserve an originary attitude, a set of dearly helds

More dear than the tawdry websites of the summoned, than the sportshops of the free, the gilded triggers of the expelled is our speech embalmed

Now like crows against snow, our eyes alone will decide
who has something to teach and who has something to learn

Alice dances the tarantella on the carpet

Between the law and the living being—the unnamable being with no nation—

is a point of imbalance, steadied by no home

Hanging from clouds, intricate environments I will come to miss

You cannot stop time. Seeking paradise, invent glass

A fever lasts much longer than thought

Time is lustful in this way

The solidity of my own flower, but who's looking

Slips up his warm imagination

Are we thinking of something better?

The debaters sell soot

To a fourteen year old girl

And the world thrives? The sky arrives, an edifying

Face—But I'm unsure of the etiquette of wearing equipment, am

Headed toward a headache

A congress of meat

A civic lyric on the house floor

Hair in the grass

Looks like smoke, like tomorrow's

Problem. Alice

Floored and crying her eyes in

All about me

The sensation of a splatter of crimson

Lively on earth, a rag on earth

May I enter

The child?

Prairie grass swings

Slow dancer under winter's tone

Touch foot to floor and laugh out the holy door

I was not

Aware of this

Bubble in my mind this touchable

Object. Is there in my split

Pen's spilt

Ink a known

Thing? All about money?

No. I've loved

Being grown, another day pointing to

Girl sleeping, lips apart, each lid as if hiding

A pearl, nothing, hands clasped around a town

Not there. Sycamore limbs

Like martyred saints thrown into the flames I carry

And adore the sunglassed glint of a teenaged boy

My curve of recurrence, the poem stills

A sky or a guy's

Shoulder, pigeon coated

Dusk, an improvisation, licentious as the

Spit on my wrist

—a polluted river; my daughter's eye—

Rag on the shelf and a brush. To the leafless out there—the lamp sends a failing

dominance—

Come in whatever I am not

sleeping for

fidgets in the chest—

I practice the body

with red implements for probing

and slices of fruit

fluid swords and light bulbs in the right places

I don't care who likes or understands my methods

Standing with women in line I used to believe myself an object

Now I have less to offer; I'm more a slogan, like Neptune, pretty far from the source

Colder morning sun rising over scattered leaves sound of cars on avenue

I experience my nausea as a robotic cartoon

As a citizen I put my two hands on the old mother's back, my thigh between

the thighs of a dad

If I have a real point to make about method, it's this:

going door to door or cracking an egg on a doll's head

affixing a Band-Aid to a seizure or triumphing for a solitary moment in bed

the true purpose of what I'm doing is not to help the young but to establish myself

as an unattainable mind or mine

You are a wonderful person, said my daughter to the back of my head

But what about my hair—I protested

falling away

That nothing is found within these drawers that we ever really needed

That the quiet in a house swims as film in its emulsion, image rising

I made a movie about my life. The opening shot a polluted river, the closing shot my daughter's eye

The opening shot a yellow wall. The closing shot a dog's black tongue

That July is the month of explosions, the month of my birth, odors and waves

I made a movie about my life. The opening shot: remnants of a meal in a room. Empty cups and bits of bread

Closing shot: that same meal untouched, salad un-tossed, coffee un-poured

In the one sex scene a man takes my face between his hands and turns it away from his own. In the one chase scene, only the wheels of cars: which the chased, which chasing?

Blue walls. strike out. fallen cake. glistening pool: I made a movie about my life.

Opening shot: the inside of my mother's mouth—closing shot her left hand, her father's ring on her unmoving finger

Figures in the trees watch over me. O figures. O

envelope

That there's nothing inside the drawer but my birth certificate, my marriage license, and the deed (clouds doing nothing). That my mothers and my other mothers learned how to drive by climbing into the front seat and letting go the brake

learned how to swim by falling off a stone. Learned to run when they got sick, to write when the law demanded it, to lie when they needed money, to slap when they were slapped, to sleep when they learned to read. Failed at numbers but won at cards. Failed at cards but won at mortality. Failed at that but won at feeding: chard and spinach behind the house

balloons soaring high for the dollar store, flags flapping yellow and red. Enemies of meadows, my mothers bought cleaning fluid, bought super-balls, mac-n-cheese, golf-club pencil sharpeners, and underwear. Enemies of the untamed, they bought lunch and carried it home. Easy to eat, it needed no utensils, no cooking, no plates, no cleaning. Lunch over, nothing to throw away, no crumbs to wipe off the table, no table

Where is Carolyn?

A close-up of water pooled on pavement gives up gray to the gray

The purple hem of her skirt—wind bends an alder to the ground (clouds doing nothing)

A body falls from a bridge, falls or is pushed, pushed or is leaping; the river takes her, neon, neon in the river, o red

And "all her care is radiant," because of how it swells in me made

Through a debilitating head-thing read:

"If denial is a river it runs through doomed societies"

Happily I type:

Dear Daughter
Here is your gift: a piece of cloth
To wrap me in

Neither transmitting nor receiving, but with a wire looped over his ear
a man attempts to define the borders of the living

In a russet suit—drinks from his red cup. Turns his face to the crowd
This is where it begins, he says, the center of the woman's body its horizon

Then the snake slid free of her cage and we could find her nowhere, though we took all the drawers out of the dressers, picked the rugs up off the floor, checked inside every shoe, behind the toilets, under the beds. When the boy returned, he sat on the bottom step and cried. We left a mouse out for the snake, left the heat lamp on, but still

she did not come "home"

—consider my identity, she might say—

—a brutal response—

And in the froth of not knowing what is up with the body, I read of the girl who cut off her hands to avoid having to marry her brother.

And in the froth of not knowing what is up with the body, I read of the girl whose father cuts off her hands to appease the Devil.

While the girl without a face, possibly a hoax, gets a new sister.

Because we are going to demo this kitchen—I think of a small body of water, its entrance and exit to and from itself. One bird showed up at the birdfeeder and one fish surfaced for a mosquito. Deep in the grocery line I was known, or merely acknowledged, as a style. I've learned nothing of codes and minimally of sweat. Forty intervening years of discipline have prepared me for failure and ignorance. Now that I birth only in dreams, the child-form will be valued according to its brevity, its brevity in time. Measured by the dial and the pendulum, measured by the tape and the expense.

The pairing of thing and non-thing is everywhere before me made visible by winter light, its short burst of brightness on the tree and around the tree is what. I said, you are now barred from uttering the words "I forgot," and he agreed, gathering his papers tearfully.

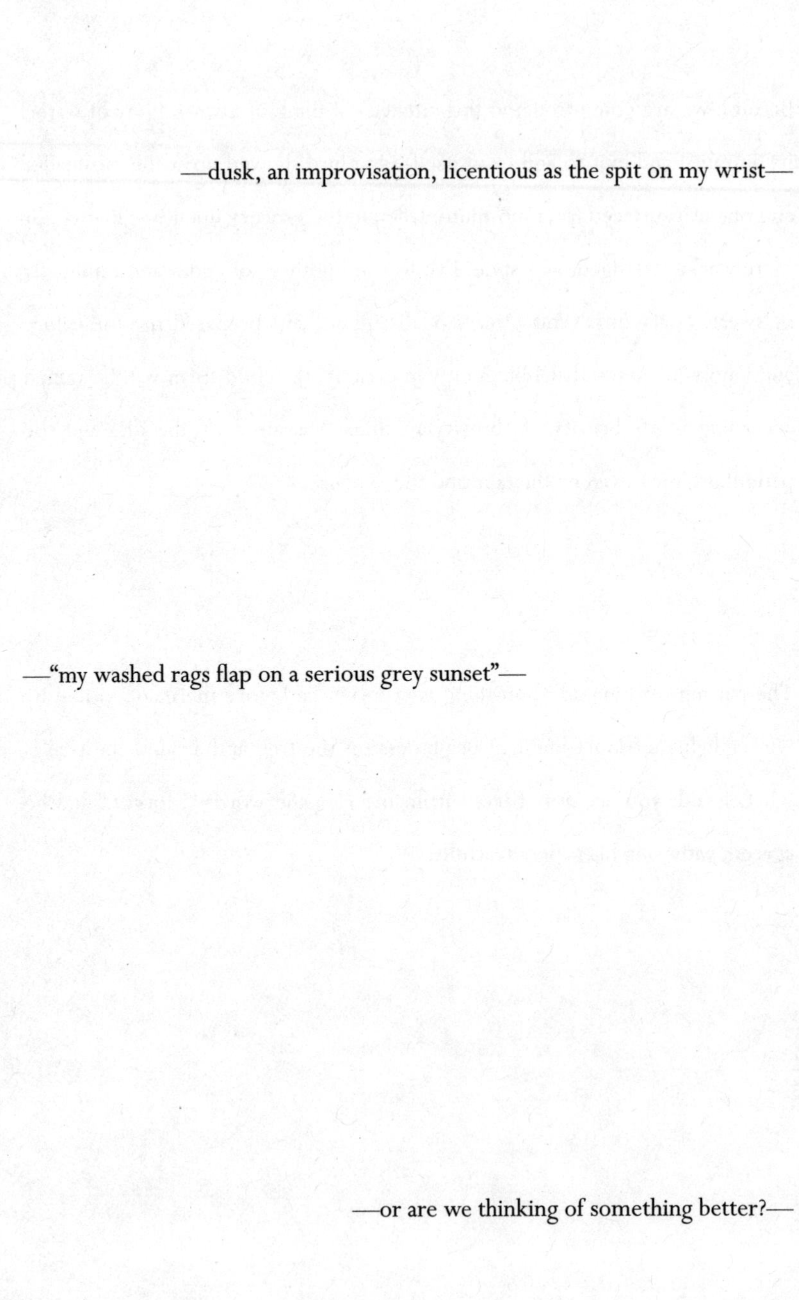

—dusk, an improvisation, licentious as the spit on my wrist—

—"my washed rags flap on a serious grey sunset"—

—or are we thinking of something better?—

Today it's like this: I am drugged under my coat and hot. The suicide book could not attract me and neither could string theory. I was attracted only by the slit in the curtain and the other drug. What is a mind that can do so much, know so little? I might give one up. The visit to the tax guy took Tuesday. Dragging his pug the flame goes out. His busy scarf lifts in a wintery spin. Next the duck pond is frozen, took the weight of five kids without comment. I thought it dicey and cautioned and grabbed for I'd read the stories of boys unable to find that hole. Thinner to the east and all the ducks convene in the one puddle remaining. Rang my searching friend to hear what she'd found. What is it to mend a mind? The site of the shooting's where Laynie shopped. Mailman's still cheery at the door with a jog.

Solid pound of meat's in the box. I've read the stories and am still a constant pulse.

—"a sort of solidarity of liquids"—

Not yet 8. Little flowers

and leaves
bob in mist

"What can it mean to me O mother / To be the one clerk

for whom nothing exists?"

The idea of something "outside"—the thirsty dark
My mother's first syllable: rose

Her last: a near inaudible: *psss   psss   psss*

—present time so fired up now?—

One woman I knew made a box in the desert and lived in it
One woman I knew watched her husband fall from a roof in Prague
One wrapped another in black cloth to protect her
A woman I knew went to Texas and bought a gun
A woman I know writes tales of the model city (a swimming shape)
One I knew felt her breasts for lumps before breakfast each day until she found one (and fed)
Made a dress out of bacon as an act of devotion to her favorite TV character (and fed)
Gathers twigs from the cemetery for her pot-bellied stove
A woman we knew wrote a treatise on love and another on dying and then she died
Put her hand inside the hose
A woman I know spent a year sleeping in bed with her daughter at the hospital
For girls who will not eat
Carries jagged scars across her right breast of which she will never speak
Raised a daughter in a movie theater
Collected dolls in an upstairs room, rising at three to dust them (a destiny)
One stands on street corners proclaiming her love for someone long gone (shadow mouth)
Another would speak of her mother's suicide only when crossing a bridge (body slum)
Buried herself in the forest standing up (body slum)
Impregnates herself to abort herself again (body slum)
One woman did not leave her apartment for twenty years (an archaism)
Moved into a bodega and lived off the foods lining the shelves
Peered out plate glass at an evolving city
A woman I knew unlocked her front door for her drug-devoted son
Handed him cash while begging him not to take it (given)
Places a forkful of meat into her mouth and will not swallow

But if poetry's sick it's because it's never enough to lie back in the snow, to let the snow fall into your mouth and eyes. All children eat like that, like they're receiving a cure.

In the tremors of sap, a sudden slump as if soft marrow there in the bone. The dying are interviewed on the radio. The shadow of a thorny branch across a furrow in the rising light's a hook like a child's call. You in your yellow shirt, a language clipped into monosyllables, a maroon carpet beneath you. Even as tree buds, a stone in the mouth of the toad, even as blood gathers in the pregnant woman's widening veins. You place your wine under your chair. Just as animals work themselves into one another, so do languages. Then scraping the gathering ice from the car, a man in March, the pivot of your heel. Our friends, recently married, and I myself, the murderer of what, or only this: if living beyond you, I will have abandoned you.

as if into one of the child's nine orifices—

But this is a vibratory nation poem—and it refers to the law
that dictates hair grow more thickly on the left side of the face than the right
(a universal truth). Prepubescent girls give off terrible smells from their soles
The "emotional body" and the "aural body" experience a huge thirst
forcing the shoulders too far forward. I'm speaking about the fertility
of Wisconsin's girls. Her mouth doubles. Her skin
a functioning product. Feeling is space slipped into time.

—Now a wind melt-down toward which we orient ourselves

as if into one of the beloved's nine orifices—

And those of us with a crush on philosophy glance into the open door
The philosophers sit sideways in their chairs—shaved heads, crossed legs, ready to fuck

The smells of Andy Warhol wind their way through the hallway
I was a boy, not a surrealist, I wanted real apples and real cheese
"Help me stop dreaming your destruction," I mouthed in the direction of his downcast eyes

What was it like
doing this?

I lived in a cathedral, not in a city; my joys were immanent

The fact is, I never much liked him peonies bloom
It was more or less my goal to ignore or hurt him peonies bloom
Being the proprietor gave me the right to do this peonies bloom
Since it was my property and everyone was my guest blooming
Variously, I disliked his smell, his hair, the shade of his skin in the spring
If the heat goes on all by itself it's not my job to turn it off folds of folds
Once I bent over and invited him to look into my asshole perky stems
Which he gladly did at the top of the stairs five fat flowers
At night I could rarely sleep and this was because of his breathing color of prom
Whatever was my general attitude, for I was full of fun the secret in the stamen
So buried was this fun in my psyche I rarely let it out eat the flower
Spurting like ketchup from a packet I cleared my throat some more spread than others
Had to sometimes sleep under him the tightest one is the one I want
The sensation of my knee against his genitals the most spread open the ugliest
On Sundays I refused to eat a thing color of girl parts
The fading petals a ball of sex unpeeled

—your fetal heat, a world unborn—

—a twist of stench in our alcohol sleep—

I had no other alternative

Being on top made for a completely new sense of being white

Now I know the money's coming in

Little, I was in love with my father

Especially on the phone

But to ventriloquize the language of the stupefied: I gave it up

I take from my pocket a packet of sugar

How familiar is a fool!

and shame my mouth on a poor girl

And disgrace my mouth on that poor girl's scars

for which I have an enormous pity

I had to do this: I'd missed it too much

We sweat out all the wilderness left in us

Consider the beautiful word "give"

And the harvest moon about to rise

But whiteness is so disappointing

Scrape eyes from the shield, ice from the glass

I can offer you no more

be no better

But now I've grown to love the rough skin. The tail of the mouse. Wrecked dollhouse. Is the cause of children a cause? What is the relationship between the brick wall, the outdoor light blinking off, and the wintering tree? Between my mother's unbreakable silence, her husband's loom, and the frozen lake we skate? Is grieving a politics? In some states it's illegal to teach the young to care more for their race than their individualism. To imagine the shape of the country differently

to imagine different borders. I do this with a sense of deadline, of the movement of time. And so am chilled. As when two prisoners share a cell and one behaves like a dog, licking, walking on all fours, barking—the other refuses to stroke his head. As when I cannot be stirred to respond to a child because the season hangs savage between us: a gloved hand lacking the motivation or maybe the capacity to remove its partner's glove, and thus its own.

The "pendulum snow"—a neighbor in the dark
of the shovel its
slightly tipped for nipple
way. Muscles directed
as by heft he flattens his
location. All this

dying laughter
after song's debasement

—made to seem industrial under fluorescence—

—she stops crying—

—her fetal heat—a world unborn

If one is to "abdicate all responsibility," to let the others do it, the others do the organizing, since one is "beyond" "bad at it"—So says the man, seated in the lounge, shrugging, apologetic, amused. A woman takes a breath, draws a circle in the corner of the page. Is it raining? It's four in the morning. Every sound swells. In the tale the oldest brother's pockets are empty, his sack is empty, his feet go round and round. Moment by moment the fountains release their upsurge as rain pocks their pools. What is happening? asks the nine-year-old. Dancers in black reveal a narrative of war. The city's roof gardens go green. Actors in tights smoke in doorways. Frowning girls read on trains. Says the man, I cannot over emphasize how much I am against this. The women uncross and re-cross their legs. Lights blaze into the night with the attitude of horses, the attitude of fruit trees by highways. My hands circle the ribs of the sleeper and lift her from the couch while he codes a plan for a city made entirely of water, city of canals and rivers, upsurge and fall. Why can't we add another day to April? asks the younger girl with the calendar before her. Because, says the mother, that's not how calendars work. A long time ago, she says, you were a kid, and now you are not and I am a kid for a long time. How does that work? The wind like an anticipated asset arrives and is quickly subsumed into itself. Says the mother, pushing the stroller, that's time, time does that. The government avoids a shutdown by "abdicating responsibility," "beyond" "bad at it." And all sides claim victory as the lawns are soaked and someone adds a six-pack of Red Bull to the bill. If one is to "take a breath" from another's mouth, moment by moment the sun will spill its blood into the basins, the gardens, the yards with their bikes and scooters, strollers, bed sheets, leashes and sticks.

Civic expenditures do not cover the tears of disappointed children whose projects win no awards or the mouths of their mothers tolerating humiliation in the auditorium as one by one winners receive medals for mastering diplomacy. I am a woman for a long time while the debt ceiling rises, the terms of my complicity braided into the tresses of my children. Our parent sameness is everywhere applauded; like the paintings in museums, we are sure of our location and are viewed. Furloughs are narrowly avoided as the nails sticking out of fences, meant for vines, vines never cultivated. Ethereal breezes stop just before reaching the brother's furrowed brow, just before adjusting his collar. And so he settles into his precise and foundational lust.

—most famished / most indolent—

—my own body / not myself—

—fixed face: redolent face—

You're finished with that, so return to the kitchen where there are always tasks in a
damp sequence

What woke me: own heat, own body as if not myself

Arrived at the party with one extra girl who had suddenly become mine

"What will happen to us? How will we feed the children when we have nothing for
ourselves?" said the woodcutter to his wife

At 3 in the morning a sound. It was my son gulping water from the faucet. It might
have been anyone

The nine-year-old shot in Arizona is not

Mine she is mine

No. Sang two songs before bed, two that she'd written for the concert in red

And coughs then: who is so mobile and so amplified?

Then I said, disobediently, I was not going to bed, no also to movies, we were not

Going to watch a movie. When I saw the killer's face, grinning from the front page

I stuffed it in a drawer. To my own face with its endless changes endless sameness its eyes

I said no. I wanted to be a hole. In the road, the garden

Dust across my keys, sugar in my teeth, to the jaw of the bus driver as I boarded the bus

I said no. Today I will not remove the isolated hair from my basin. Not figure

Some cleaner end

—her hacked face shines from her fixed face—

—so how can I place a hand there?—

Was that it then? The muscular pattern of an adult day? Slice fruit. Lift the phone and wash someone's hands. A girl, I sat in a theater. Yellow flash of light on the screen. The father was dead but I didn't get it. My father breathing beside me. Two kids walked into a desert. Dad asleep right by me. In another one, kids at school. Another one, kids on bikes. Was I watching for something to focus? Was a body. A body that was breathing.

If a man put his hand there, you'd done something to him, something bad so you could hate him. Allow me to adjust that. If a friend's father sneaks a pat, you could tell if you wanted to or just take it. In one movie two boys compete for the piano teacher's kiss. These are boys in a war and one won't make it. Woods are a place for hiding under leaves. Leaves won't do it. In another a boy sleeps with his mother. But what did that flash of yellow mean. My mother had a tongue or a temper. Does your father ever smile, one kid said. Was up in a tree or down in the mouth. Snapping heads off flowers or robbing stores. Something under my shirt to be found. If a father put his hand there you could hate him.

One boy on our couch had a mother who was dead. This was an installation. I wrote everything that mattered down. When the car flamed up, the kids walked off. When the war came, they went to a monastery. Every story gets kids alone. In the car with my father I ran out of comments. The river fled beneath the bridge to remind us about time. Was that it then? A series of smells and a long wait for what. A series of films like flashes of light. Was "sick of my face." Said my mother, ruefully, a slight roll of her eyes, "don't worry. It'll change."

That's it then, the dark theater in which I heard a father breathing, the suicide father blowing himself up before me, his car exploding into amber light. A sister and a brother walk away from that death. Little lift of her chin, blue skirt blurred by sun. Was waiting on carpets and couches—for the muscular pattern of an adult day. "Sick of my" car rides and corners of grey. The city smells of its river. Don't try so hard, said someone taking my picture in a tree.

Slept on the couch with Moby Dick in my hand, fan headed straight for my face. Might dream the past right into its present. But everything ugly destroys us. Even a rock. Some dirt. A canvas bag. The fence with its tines out of place. No "automobile" is beautiful. No "cooling unit" can be. The sky getting wracked as a teen on film. When I was one, I disdained grown men, sampling eyes.

The father pisses the beach, back to the shore. They fired him, they paid him off, his baby's trounced. A strained and faltering hand headed right for her face, her face, a mere pest of the present. Everything girly toys with that man. A gull pecks some dirt. Cold here and there, all ugly and automatic but tearful. No "leaking heart," a guy's just burning, my watching eyes like a stain on the fence, oiled even now by disgust.

Wind pulls the trigger breath, redesigned air
Chlorine gas blown into your face
The past arrives, an object

—that it then?— the—

Tired kid at the bus stop pulls her hood up. What other estrangements disguise themselves as intimacy? The hills in snow suddenly rise as if a detail of the body usually clothed

The survivor's fear of renewed persecution settles as a cough in the night. As the metallic scent of the subway, metallic voices of kids in a group

Or, the sculptural qualities of plants stun the light

Sliced a peach and found a boy inside

They had always wanted a boy

Nobody should have to travel those roads, said the man, sending him off

Avoid large places at night. Keep to small ones in the day

Their daughter they offered to the sun, but the sun said the cloud, which blotted out his face,

Was greater

So they offered her to the cloud. The cloud told them that the wind freely blew it about

They asked the wind. The wind said the wall could easily stop it. They asked the wall

Which took her

Well, said the woman, even if you don't want to be king, I want to be king

When she arrived at the sea it was dark gray

And the water heaved up from below with a foul smell

And though she was made king, all the cats, their tongues red with blood, cried in unison:

We bewitch you, so that whenever you attempt to speak, all manner of filth

Shall fall out of your mouth

And the book she loves best describes a doctor who has sex with his patients—all of them, or all the ones he can stand. The book she loves features a doctor whose taste in clothes is very good, who does not give a shit about anyone's close-up fear, a doctor who feels alive only when screwing a patient or a shop girl, until his eventual suicide.

My brother is correct, she thinks, folding the page, when he observes
this is the doctor I am.

—but I had not yet decided

—whether as a weightless scarf

or as a trailer set permanently off its wheels—

In April of 1988 the telephone fixed to the wall. A barrier between the voice of the man and my ear such that his face becomes aesthetic or perhaps prosthetic. Laundromats are erotic so I frequent them alone. Plastic seats take on the same meaning as the foam at lakeshore. In over half of all cases, a rogue girl will widen the avenue by walking it. In perilous tinny journeys she fails to locate her room.

A bare cheek stunned by the cold and some meat on the stair. Now her mouth's intricate movement accuses us of the cowardice we all share.

A bed holds a girl with her thumb in her mouth. I was thinking about movies and how men make them. Another one on the playground, directed by her friend not to play with the other friend. Where was I going with this, she thinks, walking on the avenue with her hands in her pockets and hair afloat. Nine percent of films directed by women means 91 percent directed by men. It's been raining for days. My film has no people in it, but a building spewing smoke and an ant in the dirt. Sun spread like shit over everything. My film rubs against fourteen windows and the undersides of cars. Movie of betrayal and clairvoyance, the mother's mind spilling in a cornfield. The girl in the frigid sea. I was never an addict, but I was a liar.

Or a three-year-old hovers behind a couch while her parents fight. Days and months and then she's on a train with her mother and brother headed south. Says the girl to her mother, when you die you will talk to god and you will see your friend who died, and you will be happy. Says the girl to her toys, I am so excited to get very old because then I can talk to god. Sky glowing pink behind the three-story building. At ten she makes eggs for house painters, calls up the ladders the men climb down to eat.

Blond light swells

from out the windows of abandoned buildings, rises from a hole in the ground. Was thinking about daughters with their long hair and defiance in debate club, dance class, soccer team and band. White sails drift over the river's motility.

Sunlight slapped over everything.

In the film without people: a blue sky behind branches. Snapped guardrail of a bridge. A billboard advertises nothing

but the flourish of a blush. Light swelling.

—and if I grow sick in public—

Fog skims the bit of blood between the dual embrace of my skull sides. It's like that in a tree when you're a kid looking down. The drive was long and the road uneventful. Later we'd wash the headache off.

What was it I wanted to do there in the crotch of the tree? To observe the motion of other children eating fruit? To see something about a mother whose death hung around her, fogged or forged into restlessness?

> More than anything, I was aware of my arms. And my head, not a problem.
>
> Not yet. From out of a wretched tide through the heat, mothers pass.

Woman on film bends over, the lead positions himself behind her. This is how it works, he tells her. I want you and so I know you want me, even if you do not know it. She thinks about that for a while.

> What spectacle licks our faces in theater dark?
>
> A pink—from a trench—tryst of breath and sweat.

In prose I explain to my daughter the reasons to avoid the passive voice. But why is it worse, she asks, reasonably.

—debaters sell soot—wayward in the fruits—lively on earth, a rag on earth—

—and she is the genre of infinite call—

What if time was all that was wanted?

The finally squandered evening

The movie paused and the two girls down

It's only within the house that we don't want surveillance cameras

I with my breath in my throat with its flag

Two girls unknowable. What

ever the owner wants

I want too

In the lobby of soldiers and their families, a cartoon running for kids

By this time I've relinquished my previous

But what about the stricken other woman?

Stricken land: "striken in elde"

I sat beside my son in his sickness, looking up saw the girl at the stair

It was like nothing to be sitting there like nothing at all

The dismantle of exhausted light is one way to say it one way to get old

People so universally obey the dictum of night

Dictum of piss and froth

It's nothing to be sitting here nothing

Soft and valued for softness; hard and valued for hardness

Showers in the semi-light
Flavored my mouth through evening
Effort the fingers into something
Sorry doesn't walk the dog

Dropped death plans in favor of platanos and sex
Swatted back questions and skewered insinuations
As recalcitrant and incisive as forthright and emotional
Like flowers, power chords cannot be probed
I am here to tell the truth, there is no hatred
I wait for the bus to arrive
Or sleep
Or not sleep

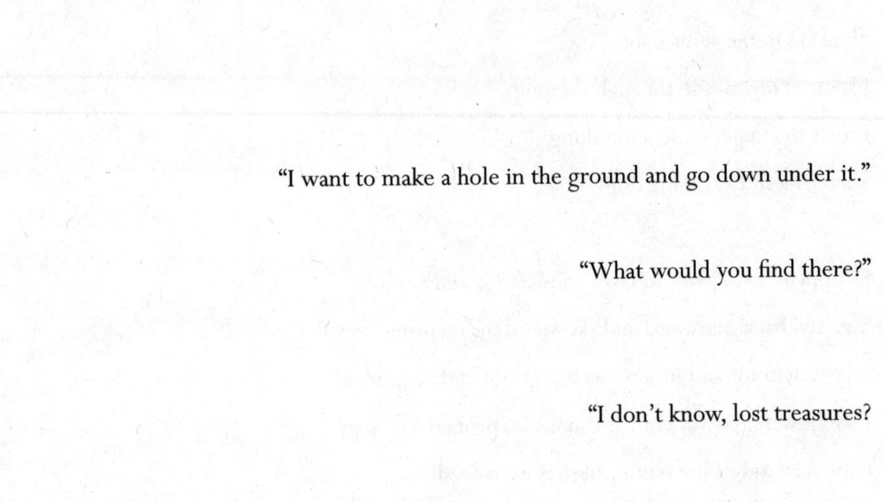

"I want to make a hole in the ground and go down under it."

"What would you find there?"

"I don't know, lost treasures?

But how do I make a hole? Tell me, I trust you."

To write against dying. Not against one's own death with its coffee colored smudge, but against the idea of cessation. And by "against" one doesn't mean in opposition to, but rather leaning on as if a wall. Just as every line in its pauses takes that breath, if you could say that, of cessation. Mixed drinks on the causeway, apple seed on the lip. Either way it's the same: one thing displays itself against another. The sun's final rays could not be seen, nor felt, nor ever really known, by anyone in this room. All sequestered in their listening, listening to the sound of her voice as she, laughing at herself and shaking her head, read her statements. It was cold in the room; many kept their coats on.

Give some ear to that. To that woman's voice without any hint of cruel in it, the passenger seat, the dark road. We were friends, one could say, "against," or leaning on, drinking. The translator's enthusiasm for his subject had a kind of sputtery appeal. He was translating a translator who became in late middle age a writer of his own, his original, words, a storywriter in his mother-tongue. The translator had a great memory, reciting passages of prose from his position at the head of the table. The waiter appeared with a plate of eggs, another glass of wine, which he promptly spilled onto my jacket. The local team was winning, so most eyes were upward receiving that pleasure. Returning home would be, always, disappointing. For who wants to enter an unlit house? Thanks, is what she would say, exiting the car, closing the car door. Night gone solid, but not the highway: flanked by risk environments, each driver a weight with breath.

—and so our disgust is final—

—effort the fingers into *something*—

Could we discard the filthy chair
the filthy flower the fallen blonde?
Could the scarred window voluminous become?
Along realms of work of what we call labor the labor of bending of training
the others, such flashes of green, bitter bright blooms
A human stands as a barrier to rivers

Stairs blue and polished
carry us into the airport
where efficient travelers and roller boards
behave discretely as cut stems
curling back their petals in the night

So our disgust is final?
Avidly we reject the stripped bodies
with hands probing genitals and eyes stilled in a stare
But is the child's pink mouth on the screen a flash of desire or disdain?
The boy wears his access in his pocket with its coin
stationed low in his fist
"On the edge of the world a long line of black trees"
"getting and spending / howling at all hours"
we listen to those lines in our sleep

—a constant pulse—

Breasting the window casing—a bowl ill with
fruits—I could say that she is not dead
is almost a sky that I know well
"She used to send me down to the cow barn to collect the milk"
Bees rise in the lace, flies pounce the pane
hydrangea—touching no one, and I have no need to be touched

Eight years—since she found herself
gradually mindless—"She entered the hospital and returned without the baby.
Where is the baby, we asked?"—
Why is mother-love such a recurrent theme
in novels and films? "There are lovely meals waiting for you in the dining car," etc.

None of this moves us exactly
But she is the genre of infinite call

—of chancy spirit—

He steps into the basement, seats himself behind his loom. There is no one who escapes suffering. For the man "walking" his wife, there's no cure.

It's not true that water adores you. Or that memory finishes what it begins. Vagrant trees, rolling seclusions—sporty murmurs of plot

Grating future-years: let the moon prefigure death

not us

That night the porch light left on: Lure. Sun

Then, passing your own reflection in that window

and here and there an apple core, a gum wrapper, a receipt, a sweatshirt, a

            CD, a raisin, stub of a pencil, marble and crumb, sock

After recalling the need to gather, to gather at the Capitol with children

and neatly retying your shoe and exhaling

of chancy spirit

cut

Here the house grew still

as if against a heavy wind

from the north where the best parties are

and all the avenue's headlights blur

rivery but sourceless. I have not been

myself lately. Myself lately

fouled by proximity

At three a child will talk to a fish, to the stuffed

Animals. Not, but almost, sleeping

At four she wishes to avoid such errors

While before the screen Christina is seated

With her shoulder curved making deals with time

For this moment is royal

For they at the scene of it: swelling into howling and ground

At the corner of 17th and Colorado, immediacy is in the front seat

And the glare: a world ceases

On 17th Avenue the body of a girl

And the glare—a world

This royal

Stop

Recent shallows dry

up the swift

air so compatible with

face it wants

to measure my lips but my fragmented

face cannot adjust itself

into fruit or

yolk

Neck of the

kid lies

as dirt

does so

still

—document of my intentions—

—Stop—

That we were drinking at the table
blue walls receding
my worry was for the women
who live alone now without children
Dog in the cold belly to the ground
The danger of solitude is
By nine the walls had darkened
I arrived at the doorway with salt
my fist steady inside my hand
for a woman who walks with her daughter
and watches the eyes of the men
is a woman whose glance is harder
than the glance from the eyes of those men
By nine the walls were darkening
Heavy clouds staying put without rain
Car doors slamming on headlights
Dog's belly cold to the ground
What sends itself outward is turmoil
reveals the straddled fissures
in which the animal is most lazy and most circular
Glint of the knife on the counter
And a feast day arrives to dull it
while drivers consider their destinations
My worry was for the woman
made to seem industrial under fluorescence

with her back to me her waiting skin
Her torso remained as a grid
a grid with hidden charge points
Hauling wood I felt the ordinary pairing
of my breasts as if pockets held coins
old and heavy currency
and no way to spend it
A mind may be perfectly
permeable not unlike
a forest canopy
scatters light and shade
At nine the walls darkening
Tired wasp bumping the window
Between her top lip and her bottom
no landline no link
no account
And drivers considered their destinations
So I recalled her fear
In the passivity of belonging to an order
she was the first disappearing term
The more others are heard the more she is lost
And drivers consider their destinations
consider their destinations to be worthy

—thoughts wired to, slathered in, time—

—on the whip—

Yet this intimacy remains alien

as I must remember to look at the face

before it is too late and there is no face

—may I enter/the child?—

Then the mother took the little boy, put him into the pot, and cooked him into a stew. Marlene stood by crying, and her tears fell into the pot, so that the stew needed no salt—a sudden slump of soft marrow there in the bone—

The father came home, sat down at the table and said, "Where is my son?" And the mother served up a large dish of stew. "Oh," said the mother to his warm imagination, "he has gone across the country." "What is he doing there? He did not even say good-bye to me." With that he began to eat—as if into one of the nine orifices—

"Wife, this food is delicious. Give me some more." And the more he ate the more he wanted, throwing all the bones under the table—white and arching like the sincerity of summer heat—

Marlene went to her chest of drawers, took her best silk scarf, gathered the bones from beneath the table, tied them up in her scarf, and carried them outside, crying tears of blood.

She buried the bones beneath the juniper tree. (Or are we thinking of something better?)

Then the tree began to move—how power moves when hidden underground.

The branches parted, then joined together again—as if casting and recasting the inside of the body—

At the same time a mist seemed to rise from the tree, and the center of this mist burned—limitless seasonless fire—a bird flew out of the fire singing magnificently—Figures in the trees watch over us

O figures. O envelope—

It flew high into the air, and when it was gone—her own body as if not herself—the cloth with the bones was no longer there.

What night cold figure of failure—the dying laughter—

And merrily she went into the house, sat down at the table, and ate—

“Death—tho’soever Broad,

Is just Death, and cannot increase—”

I know something much scarier than death, the mother said. What is that? asked the girl.

My own brain out, said the mother, and my body

intact.

—when speaking about the nation—

—her mouth does double—

—dusk, an improvisation: a chaos/ritual—

Trees burgeon into a man is said to have murdered his wife
These little birdcalls at dawn with a knife

The lips are a seal over the mouth, an imperfect seal, thin, unreliable
The sky is an illusion. No sky

The within is red, glistening, mobile
Small shank, hammered flat and money

Is like that: glistening and mobile, a seal, unreliable
Like pigment and hormones and voice

Like pigeon and crow and quail
Smears of mud on the underside

There on the door molding, the shank lay hidden for years

The wet unlit core of the body wants to be chosen to brush
Against a party dress or a dirty corset for a man

In April I wish it not April the old
Movement of figures falling back into their cars

A decade later, the shank placed into the drawer of a desk
The face is an illusion, an illusion of presence

Form of the mouth is not

Inwardly, a tongue swells and shrinks, rests and presses, tightens without warning

Tastes of its own secretions

The skin is an illusion of containment o clothing, corset, thin, unreliable

Settles on the body as the bird skims the air

Shank in the desk drawer, desk passed between siblings, across states

Sleep, sleep, the landscape sex shop the cork like a cock the bottle neck's so tight

I hope you understand said the note found in a pocket of her dress

Morning traffic is not yet, is not yet a secretion or a tale or a crime

Billing myself as a shine I was so nervous

The turning of the earth with its cats so noiselessly crafting their descent

Salt in a dish, salt skin, the salt tears on the meat o sleep

Gray blue of the runner's shadow get down under it

Said the boy, I'm interested in tight clothing, in containment and his hands go into

His pockets to find what there what thinning

Heat like April so paved

The face is an illusion like a letter or a constellation, and what is more

Abstract in its display?

—my car/my color/and my—

—spirit cut—

Is lustful is time is

a splatter of crimson

lively on earth

Present time so fired up so

famished so indolent—

on the whip

Red in the flash drive in fractured cloud

The dismantle of exhausted light: one way to say it one way to fall

as a body from a bridge

falls or pushed, pushed or is leaping, leaping or diving—that river will take her

neon: neon in the river so red

This book is for:

Buffy Barfoot, Christina Battle, Linda Brennan, Laynie Browne, Sommer Browning, Serena Chopra, Liz Claire, Gillian Conoley, Kim Drain, Louise Elving, Sara Falk-Mann, Jessica Fisher, Anna Grace, Carolyn Grace, Claire Grace, Lyn Hejinian, K.J. Holmes, Fanny Howe, Susan Jennings, Ruth-Ellen Kocher, Jeanne Liotta, Sara Marshall, Rusty Morrison, Linda Norton, Jennifer Pap, Claudia Rankine, Lisa Robertson, Margaret Ronda, Selah Saterstrom, Eleni Sikelianos, Carol Snow, Jean Valentine, Anne Waldman, Brooke Wear, Sue Zemka, Rachel Zucker…

and in memory of

J. Kathleen Carr, Beulah Elving, Margaret Metzger, and Lillian Robbin

ACKNOWLEDGMENTS

Thank you to the editors of the following journals and websites for including some of these poems in early forms:

Volt, *Sun's Skeleton*, *Boston Review* (online), *Dear Navigator*, *A Public Space*, *Sentence*, *Mark Amerika: Remix the book*, *Titmouse*, *Columbia Poetry Review*, *New American Writing*

Thank you to Noah Eli Gordon and Andrew Zawacki for astute editing. And an enormous thank you to Rusty, Ken, and Cassie for all of it.

"In crayon drawings" is for Christina Battle. "I had thought" is for Kent Puckett. "A fever lasts" is for Tim Roberts. "Because we are going to" is for Benjamin Roberts. "Those of us with a crush…" is for and from CA Conrad. "Tired kid at the bus stop" is for K.J. Holmes. "If one is" is in memory of Akilah Oliver. "Could we discard" is for Gillian Conoley. "He steps into" is for John Grace. "That we were drinking" is for Linda Norton. Thank you to Luther Price for the use of his artwork for the cover.

FILMS, TEXTS

13: "I was drinking...": Hannah Weiner, *Open House*

16: "My purple well": Emily Dickinson, "A solemn thing—it was—I said"

19: "And all your care is radiant": Keston Sutherland, *The Odes to TL61P*

25: "Like a maelstrom with a notch": Emily Dickinson, "'Twas like a Maelstrom, with a notch"

32: "And what is knowledge in this condition?": Lyn Hejinian, *The Book of 1,000 Eyes*

33: "And so I began to consider history": Anne Carson, *NOX*

34: Lines in response to Robyn Schiff's poem "Gate"

39: References David Lean's film: *Brief Encounter* and Kent Puckett's essay "Celia Johnson's Face"

42: References the tales "The Peasant's Wise Daughter" and "Penta with the Chopped off Hands"

57: "If denial is a river it runs through doomed societies": Charles Blow, *The New York Times*, 12.16.2011

62: "My washed rags flap...": Anne Carson, "Sunday"

64: "a sort of solidarity of liquids" : Tim Morton; "What can it mean to me, Oh Mother...": Apollinaire; "The idea of something 'outside'": Jessica Fisher; "The thirsty dark": Judith Goldman; "Your mother's first syllable": Brenda Hillman

66: "Shadow mouth": Jed Rasula; "Body slum": Eleni Sikelianos

71: "Those of us with a crush on philosophy": poem derived from the language of CA Conrad; italicized and quoted lines are direct quotes

76: References Hans Fallada's *Every Man Dies Alone*, English translation by Michael Hoffman

77: “Pendulum Snow”: Emily Dickinson, “A clock stopped”

85: References Nicolas Roeg’s *Walkabout*, and Louis Malle’s *Au revoir les enfants*

91: References Rikki Ducornet’s *Netsuke: a novel*

105: “On the edge of the world a long line of black trees”: Gillian Conoley, “Hitchcock”; “getting and spending / howling at all hours”: Wordsworth, “The world is too much with us”

107: “She entered the hospital and returned without the baby. Where is the baby, we asked?”: Claudia Rankine, *Don’t Let Me Be Lonely: An American Lyric*

109: References Wordsworth’s “Tintern Abbey”

119: References the tale “The Juniper Tree”

121: “Death—tho’soever Broad, / Is just Death, and cannot increase—”: Emily Dickinson: “Suspense—is Hostiler than Death—”

125: “my color / my car / my”: Charles Olson, *The Maximus Poems*

photo by Tim Roberts

Julie Carr is the author of *Surface Tension: Ruptural Time and the Poetics of Desire in Late Victorian Poetry* and four previous books of poetry, including *100 Notes on Violence* and *Sarah-Of Fragments and Lines*. She is the co-director of Counterpath in Denver and teaches at the University of Colorado, Boulder.

RAG
by Julie Carr

Cover text set in Minion Pro and Perpetua Std.
Interior text set in Perpetua Std.

Original cover art by Luther Price, "Earthly Delights," 2012, courtesy of
Luther Price, Callicoon Fine Arts, NY, and CIRCUS, Berlin.

Cover and interior design by Cassandra Smith

Offset printed in the United States
by Edwards Brothers Malloy, Ann Arbor, Michigan
on 55# Enviro Natural, 100% recycled, 100% PCW
Acid Free Archival Quality FSC Certified Paper
with Rainbow FSC Certified Colored End Papers

Omnidawn Publishing
Richmond, California
2014